Green Man

ALSO BY JOHN DONLAN

Domestic Economy (1990, 1997)

Baysville (1993)

Green Man

John Donlan

poems

RONSDALE PRESS

GREEN MAN
Copyright © 1999 John Donlan

RONSDALE PRESS LTD.
3350 West 21st Avenue
Vancouver, B.C., Canada
V6S 1G7

Set in New Baskerville: 11 pt on 13.5
Typesetting: Julie Cochrane
Printing: Hignell Printing, Winnipeg, Manitoba
Cover Design: Julie Cochrane
Back Cover Author Photo: Dean Sinnett

Ronsdale Press wishes to thank the Canada Council for the Arts, the Government of Canada through the Book Publishing Industry Development Program (BPIDP), and the Province of British Columbia through the British Columbia Arts Council for their support of its publishing program.

CANADIAN CATALOGUING IN PUBLICATION DATA

Donlan, John
  Green man

  Poems.
  ISBN 0-921870-66-3

  I. Title.
PA8557.O536G7 1999   C811'.54   C99-910413-6
PR9199.3.D66G7 1999

for
Miriam Clavir

ACKNOWLEDGEMENTS

The author gratefully acknowledges the following publications in which poems in *Green Man* first appeared: *The Antigonish Review, Canadian Literature, Event, The Fiddlehead, Grain, The Literary Review of Canada, The Malahat Review, Off the Shelf, Poetry Canada, The Word Enamel.*

The financial support of the Banff Centre for the Arts, the British Columbia Arts Council and the Canada Council for the Arts greatly assisted the writing of this book.

Thanks for advice, support and example to Roo Borson, Don Coles, Judith Fitzgerald, Don McKay, Erin Mouré, Sharon Thesen, Rhea Tregebov, David Zieroth and Jan Zwicky.

The cover image of the Green Man is from a photograph by Clive Hicks of a corbel in the church of Saint Jerome, in Llangwm, Monmouthshire (Gwent), probably 15th century. Reproduced from *The Green Man: The Archetype of Our Oneness With the Earth*, by William Anderson, published 1990 by HarperCollins.

CONTENTS

Green Man

He doesn't fear much: great parts of his life
live beyond the pleasure principle.
Laws fill his veins, and laws kill him.
He'll drive up through pavement to meet his needs
without worrying if he's happy or not.
"When heads won't work, bodies must serve."
He doesn't care what will stop him: fills space
around him with creation, builds a room
of leaves and light, open.

Even those plaguey monks — illiterate moles,
pig-ignorant, copying by rote —
could squeeze a drop of sap from their dry cells
to foliate a corner of the word.

And ancient, all scarred bark, their little lungs
a ragged green hanky one arm waves
above a ravaged trunk, trees' dowager dignity
commands a moment's calm: they hold time there
in a rough column, its monument.

Winds that blow through us, that blow around the world,
stir us deep, to our great cracked hearts — storms
of emotion: Van Morrison singing "Madame George";
someone looking through photographs, saying to himself,
"This was your wife; you have no wife any more."

Rock-solid in earth, we spread our arms
in love's dumb function; high up from harm,
in punky-soft dark cavities cauterized
around old damage, warm creatures can shelter.

6 October 1992

Lever

Flowing, flowing, the energy dance: my heart
lubs along, rattling the walls, learning
its room, panther; or pacing important traffic
in the stalk joining parent and child, the link
between the breather and the world of air.

Dam:
guardian of awful energy, penstock pointing
power at a turbine, saying, Move.

With a Why-won't-ye. What hand controls,
fathers the act? Mine alone? That god's
who gripped my wrist on our rare walks, afraid
I'd escape like a dog or pig? No sir:
the siren hemorrhaging to Emergency,
the sparrow screaming in the she-cat's jaws,
the silent gull's underwing, sunset-red —

all there is today takes a hand
in what I do, untethered in my field.

19 August 1992

Out of It

Hot knives, Thai sticks, boomers, spliffs,
beer after beer after beer, pitchers of it,
wine — a litre at least — drunk beyond taste,
chemical: you were like a tree
trying to be only bark.

Formed the habit of escape early; then learned to love
your long fall back into the world. Seduced
by the hollow draw of empty air, your chest
fluttered and thrilled at lofting down
one last surrendering flight.

So here you stand, grounded — still entering down
into the body you must love as much
as each aloof attainable mountain. They
shoulder your feet like allies
while you contain, and choose to live on, air.

25 May 1993

Artifact

He bicycles through the cemetery little thinking
of these grave dead who, startled, shocked, or pining ready,
                                        stopped
one day and never moved. He doesn't know
their stories, nor make them up. Rather he senses
a universal, a particular;

that polished granite: how long will it shine?
This white stone's become all runnelled and pocked
from rain with car exhaust in. Orange burst
of lichen — he doesn't want to be dead
and will be. Oh bite that.

No wonder he so intently studies
evidence of wear and weathering;
nowhere else is proof so clear
time happens to matter.
Still he's not stone.

25 May 1993

A Sod

He has mountain fatigue. They're all around.
His energy is high, he's tired
of town, impatient with what in him isn't mountain.
If he could peel away all those hours of watching TV,
make himself better —

Some bug-nature in him,
dumb, driving,
indifferent to reason, maniacally motivated,
works unrelenting. It's essential,
yet part of him despises that bug.

Clouds are dusting the high slopes with snow,
frosting the dark green conifers almost colourless.
How long would it take to get up there?
No bug could, in a lifetime. His long legs . . .
No. Accept their distance. Hello, bug.

22 May 1993

Uncover

He cried, the whole core
of him shook and loosened.
Fears he'd remain Jello or puddle didn't
come true. Still got a body
with bones, boy.

Old wrongs he felt through to trembling, purged and finished
with. They formed him. Still he seeks
what lacked.
Occasionally fondles melancholy,
lost loves, comfort in familiar slump,

or jolts his pulse with operatic
scenes from wish, from memory. Fondly
oversees and does not chide
these nervous leaps off the starting-block,
coaches his ongoing stride.

26 May 1993

Immune

Post-fever, his mind hovers and drifts,
regrowing connections through the burnt clearings.
Work, friends, home are rooted bases
in floating muskeg. He's tussock-hopping
through what he doesn't want to lie down in,

what wants to take him under.
There's an order below the will and grasp
of consciousness. Its dark laws frighten him
when delirium looses despair to raven in
the tightening spiral of lost options.

At his body's deep response, viruses melt.
Hope is a chemical he replicates,
learning to trust the tough enduring mat
thriving in continuing decay,
living into the fabric he is made of.

25 May 1993

Milkweed

for Rhea Tregebov

He wishes he were welcome on earth as milkweed
in its fat time, sticky with life.
Turn of summer, swelling flesh-white pods
dry, go grey, and let fly down the wind
fragile immortal legions carrying

the locked code of their futures.
He's filling gaps, rewriting his own instruction manual.
"To dwell on past injuries is not good for the self."
This from a woman whose people were inhaled like smoke
into the extermination camps of Europe.

She lives beyond survival. He learns, welcomes
that wider choice, a world of breathing room.
Burning off some bit of undigested
twisted history, he hikes the river trail.
One voice says, "Watch your step," and one says, "Slip."

1 June 1993

Plunge Pool

Wet with sweat and spray, he follows the canyon
the river chews back into history.
Here free-falling water's
profoundly confused, rebels in all directions
scouring its pot of rock.

Something too familiar about this hollow
full of roaring.
Good thing it's geography, not just some metaphor
for states of mind and body whose awful pounding
no soundness can survive.

"Intelligence is one part of the mind controlling another;
instead of fighting, it's best if the bad part
gives up." Let's go. One more hour's effort
opens into a clearing, the river nearly level.
The trail down passes the falls again.

5 June 1993

Wear

for Miriam Clavir

Her heart warms, takes a shine
to the smooth gleam on objects of human use,
the polish of repetition.
Climbing steps whose lips are worn to curves
she knows the comfort of the familiar,

the marks of a loving choice made and remade.
"Testimony to a life well lived, well served."
Explain, explain. Water
flows down, makes and prefers its channels.
We've been here. We do this. We continue.

No place we've been well touched shows the trace.
Some currents of our inner ocean
follow the first hand that set them moving.
Some run free as they were born. Some eddy and whirl:
the clumsy thumbprint on the Monarch's wing.

5 July 1993

Blotter Eyes

Sorrow, that greedy cowbird,
hunts and feeds on blotter eyes,
too-mothering mothers who let anyone in
to crowd the nest and gobble pleasure.
He's caught himself in supermarkets

scanning faces for the code, for
those eyes tender with injury.
Mirrors, he realizes, mortified.
What did he expect? What could they do
but reflect grief?

In self-defense he looks away
to end the phantom opera.
A sober confrontation in the glass
stops confusion multiplying. It makes clear
who wants comfort, who can provide.

2 August 1993

Geranium Lake

Signposts and maps impose some Shewfelt's name
on *my* Shoefelt Lake's soft footprint in the rock.
Water lilies clutter the shallows, memorizing
the truth of falling light.
Nights they enfold their beauty like a yolk.

A frog chances the surface. Those ripples
fracture the wavering sky and centre him
like a target. A pike takes him down.
In reedy silence striped yellow, green, and black
frog becomes pike.

A tube of Geranium Lake displays one star
for Permanence, where some pigments carry four.
Van Gogh was fond of it. It recalls him
faintly, pale with years of maintaining
its red identity, containing so much blue.

15 August 1993

Island

No hydro lines anywhere. Wild sheep
wheel jerkily and clatter out of the yard,
trailing dirty skirts of fleece. Outside the orchard
two little deer squabble over an apple.
Seals watch us from the reef.

Tempting to let the clock run down,
to feel the hands of season after season
shape us like dough.
Deep in the second growth littered with car hulks,
bread rises in woodstoves.

On the mainland, clearcuts metastasize
into neighbourhoods.
We see the way we cultivate
our heart of wildness in how they thrive,
our lots, our parcels of still-breathing earth.

24 September 1993

Our Mothers

(On my birthday)

Cheerfully hated, helplessly loved,
we carry them "beneath our heart"
until a day they appear quite separate:
involuntary, they slip the bond and are
their own women, ordinary, like us.

How long we had gone on giving them
such magical powers! They were huge
for us, nearly invisible
beyond the focus of power and need
so long as what they gave us was ourselves.

"Damn!" shocks us from our trance
into a room echoing with a woman
sewing, rubbing her thumb, pricked.
A frown, a rueful smile at hurt
fading: no one we know.

26 October 1993

Witness

A form of the truth, and all we have
of what really happened. The way it was,
decreasingly graspable, more easily shaped
and coloured each time we reconstruct it.
A leaf sinking into the mould of leaves.

"Getting perspective" we call it, when the rush
of experience washes back to sea
and, dripping and peering out, we say,
"The following took place." The muddled tenses
confirm that history is in the making.

Evidence is what we have kept and made ours,
what the observer captures in the web
of identity and devours into language.
Yet an unspeaking part of us can see
beyond the net, the brother creature flying free.

15 November 1993

Goodbye

The chain of husk-growings and sloughings-off
starts with an itch below the skin.
The armour around feeling thickens beyond utility,
numbs him to hazard or care.
The world lessens.

Like a child left alone in the dark
he has lost touch.
His outside is all made from himself.
"See me; feel me . . . " The body's lack
swells in an annihilating wave.

He tears free, leaving intact a hollow
papery skin. Touchy, newly brilliant,
the muscular escape artist winds through
jewel-sharp blades in his familiar jungle,
hunting. He sips the million-scented air.

3 January 1994

Ghosts

Why does he daily reconstruct
false selves? Against all evidence
they belittle and criticize.
It's as if the bright facts of each day
corrode in sleep,

                where from a secret grave
a glass-encased pope rules;
a staring zombie-wolf, gripped by the nape,
must memorize a catalogue of pain.
They survive the sunrise. Will and hope

are sabotaged by buried grief and rage.
The gothic drama he contains
is a sad family
whose tenderest member shares the hurt
his teachers were too young to bear.

9 February 1994

Happiness

"The poet already had what she wanted, and mere happiness would have made a poor exchange. "
— Claudia Roth Pierpont

How strangely level a full life seems
after a habit of solitude's
dimly felt unvoiced extremities.
Nothing is lacking; desire pines
for absence, restless, like a cat circling to sleep.

What is this not-enough that is always here?
How tired you will be tomorrow
you don't care, wanting to stay awake
past fatigue. Like a drowsy child gripping a treasure,
you won't release the day.

You are unwilling to fall into a dark
whose end might be a day where all is changed
past what you believe is bearable; or where
you must endure kindness over and over
until your armour wears away.

1 March 1994

Mug

Those seamless childhood leaps into daylight —
across the vertiginous crevasse
between sleep and waking —
falter. A morning abyss
widens with the blows that make you wary

of the sun's inexorable creep.
They crack your life. You don't know
what you lack: consoling, or direction.
You learn to shade your inmost colours
from the glare that bleaches eggshell-white.

Yesterday's coffee grounds go in the compost,
you mull over the scraps of last night's dream,
let them settle into memory
in the dim quiet before you act,
drink from your crazed old favourite, still whole.

18 March 1994

Leicester

for Philip Larkin

Towards the city centre, off New Walk
a rectangle of sky has opened up
where something old was torn (you'd say pulled) down.
You'd know what had stood there, and curse
if you were alive. You'd be, what, seventy-two?

Workers are pouring concrete for the piers
of what will squat on the tamped, narrow ground
they've seen and handled so often each square inch
— yellow chert, dark marl, red bits of brick —
is as familiar as if it were their own.

That daily closeness is as good as love,
good as the heart's delighted rushing out
to unexpected heaven. By the park
a blind woman unchains her dog to run —
each looking up, with an intake of breath.

29 March 1994

Memento

for Ayrton Senna

Death, murmuring below the skin
can be so forcibly importunate
on the right direction of a life
as to paralyze the will; and then he grins
grimly back at despair, his living face.

Behind the mirrored mask
excitement judders:
the machine wants this
energy locked, to feel its power rise
fighting the brake.

Containing pent-up time
in the pit, it strains
to ride the instant's line into a curve
as fine as nerve; to be
faster than thought, letting the future crash.

14 June 1994

Lions

Subdivisions loop and scythe the green
slopes of mountains blackly capped with rock
like broken teeth ("the Lions" — as if things were
de-fanged by naming), snow-streaked in July,
rust-tinted through miles of traffic haze.

Imperial animals must have comforted
whoever agreed "They *do* look like lions,"
who'd never seen one, nor the "home" country,
parent-powerful, tiny with distance,
safe in the imagination.

When Eddy was left alone all day, poor dog,
he'd build himself a kind of memory-nest
on the rug, of whatever smelled of us:
books, bedding, a fur hat, a toilet brush . . .
How seldom we wish to be completely here.

5 July 1994

Picture

for Gary Brownlee

They were wild childhoods
beside the swamp: half-animal, we ventured
deeper where roots lifted their knees
from dark ponds further darkened where our fathers
had poured crankcase oil.

Up on Church Hill big kids threatened
to cut off our dicks unless we'd run
so they could hunt us with pellet guns. A slug
hit Gab over the eye. They let us go
if we'd lie for them. We had stonefights

in the gravel pit: missiles whirred
thrillingly near our heads like hummingbirds.
We all remember. Betty hanged
herself while her baby cried. No one knew how
to stop. Stop the picture.

26 September 1994

Clearcut

for Jan Zwicky

Serviceable and dead
the scarred, ink-blackened surface of this table
remembers its moist forest. In the grain
I sight-read bird-cries, the rests and stops
of its vivid, vanished inhabitants.

They're gone and I survive.
I mourn, and try not to will on myself
that dark silence that's swallowed them. Guilty
of the hard fact of life at their expense
I share their elemental appetite.

So, not so very wicked. See, the yard
is rich with laurel, holly, cherry, pear —
shelter. And trays of seed rewind the feathered
clocks whose clicks and chirpings soothe my fear
of the day when they won't sing, or I won't hear.

18 October 1994

Starmap

What I've given up, so many times,
when it all could have been solid and safe:
steady job, an apartment, friends
in a town I was getting to know.
They would begin to grow smaller

as if I were already flying away from them.
Their stable base nourished my strength
to carry, on this vital migration,
the necessary balance of sorrow
and the freedom of being unknown.

They comfort me,
these parcels old as my life. They hold
people, animals, places
dear from first memory. Lovingly I fold
the cloth once more over their faces.

20 October 1994

Way to Go

Hanging flames of cherry leaves
dull and wink out in the grass. Our eyes
and some inner, lower current are lured
when maples shake exhilarating
flurries loose with each gust.

Frail bright ones slacken their hold
on the earth as it leans
from the sun and grows colder.
Deep things settle and breathe slower,
eased from the demands of light.

Despite the lip service paid
to wakefulness, we welcome sleep's change.
We all want the fall:
to say goodbye
provided we stay.

8 November 1994

Mosaic

Who is this love song for
I wonder. I'm kneeling on the floor
suddenly crying to the cat. "Oh Sammy,
we've lost a lot of people." He comes near
and bumps against my head.

This mother's music for her Three Babies,
her voice bare and true to all our sorrows,
recalls me from an arid zone
into my own dark water.
Who is lost?

The soul, wandering beyond the body,
weeps for reunion.
It homes on a remembered sound:
an infant playing on a reedy shore
still unconscious of its solitude.

30 December 1994

Opera

for Ethel Donlan 1907–1995

The juncos are having none of it.
The birds, black-hooded, fix their reptile gaze
on the main chance, feasting on bugs
on sawn-off branches, and in the flowering tree.
It's a jumble out there: amputated limbs

litter the yard.
Sinuous and segmented as worms,
green with the greens of lichen, moss, and mould,
they are still living. Watered, in a vase,
they will continue, briefly, to bloom.

Until your spirit was overcome
by your wrecked body, you loved to see
(I can still hear your voice
swerve towards song with happiness)
these beautiful shamelessly showy pink pompoms.

19 April 1995

High Falls

The north branch of the Muskoka River
airborne, falling
ten metres over its granite dyke
Eehaw! Get *down!*
each sparklet glitters and roars.

Listening;
no clear idea who is addressed;
middling acquainted with myself
lichen-rooted in this Shield
landscape, nature's janitor,

I pick human stuff off the trail:
Molson Canadian bottle-cap maple leaf,
glass blades in wait for animal feet,
double-flanged polyvinylsomething shard
— not the moth wing fallen to needle duff, dissolving.

27 August 1995

Flirt

People are such flirts. Their animal spirits
rise and quit their dreary doppelgängers
as easily as you'd leave a chair.
I've given up even trying to figure that out:
these tracks were laid for a lot of trains to run on —
maybe escape is in our nature.
Attention, like a dog slipped from a leash,
leaps away from the body's drag of grief
out the window, heading for the trees.
Or it roots around in a parent's box of keepsakes,
sorting a scrappy inheritance
   as if that could close a valve on sorrow,
   as if we were as brave as that plum tree
   and could feel her leaves yellow and fall.

25 October 1995

Tilt

Dear body, snow fell many miles
as if to be with you today.
The river with its ruff of ice reminds you
to protect the warm column of blood
around your voice — the voice you sometimes feel
there is no use for.
Dear body, the birds have voices, don't they?
So let's not have any more nonsense of that sort.

You love surface geology: here —
take this slope anchored in pines and grasses,
this jacked-up slab of crumbling sea-floor we call Mountain;
wear the earth as if it was your skin.
Don't forget you have that wet red muscle
pushing heat to your limits, dear body,
beyond any extremity you know.

31 October 1995

Coelacanth Clouds

Mule deer moving across rough country:
cartilage slides smoothly in its socket.
The wind's voice, translated through the low
hiss of pine needles, says, "You belong."

Overhearing, you're unsure
of your inclusion: you're used to hearing the wind say "Die,"
chiselling away at concrete towers.

Here it scours grains of mountain ice
against the rock face, perfectly indifferent.
Two ravens play in its upward rush as if
celebrating gravity's overthrow:
fly up like bingo balls, drop like rags,
soar where prehistoric fish once swam
suspended above the ocean bed. They glance
sidelong at you, tumble and call. You laugh
to see such sport. Coelacanth clouds drift by.

21 November 1995

EAST
VAN

For Mir

Satellite of Peace . . . Remember our relief
over Sputnik — clunky metaphor
for parental empires finally warring safely
distant in outer space?

We too compete by remote control:
who gets the most interesting mail?

Our lonely mothers ached to hear their child
speak. We couldn't say what they needed most
to hear: we were not men, and so we failed them.

We are with each other more like the pair
of eagles courting in flight over VanTerm:
sure in our element, and in our friend.

26 March 1996

Big Mind

A fingernail catches on the cracked glaze
of a cup; rare snow
lies along the veins of plastic-looking laurel leaves.

When the self feels no more present
in the whole span of one's attention
than that catch or snow

the world moves smoothly in this body,
igniting pheromones, gladhanding cupped receptors
welcoming it, particle and wave;

photons, macromolecules: the world's substratum
interpenetrates like the memory
of someone loved, beyond recovering.

What is the secret you won't tell yourself,
your life an engine for generating life?

20 April 1996

Ignorant Song

I don't know, I don't know.
High puffy clouds are blowing in from the sea,
blowing by, and the sky clears, blue.

Cherry petals whirl down, a pink blizzard,
until the back yard is more pink than green.

Now the roofers arrive
and stack bundles of red asphalt shingles.

Hard labour. Randy pauses for breath.
The sound of petals against the window.

2 May 1996

For Tu Fu

A cloud spills over the forested crest
of Grouse Mountain, and the Two Sisters beyond
are entirely hidden. How dark it must be
there in black rock and snow. Downtown the sun

glares off the city's towers and backyards.
The great port of Vancouver and many miles
lie between us yet I imagine clearly
gravel, the rock, the mist, and no one there.

High above, tendrils of the bright edges of clouds
extend and dissolve into a blue
an eagle suddenly traverses, so distant
it might be any bird, except for its speed and stillness.

4 July 1996

———

"Everything's Going My Way"

Reading poems of the Chinese masters
I envy their mountain sanctuaries.
I wish that rich ancient silence would stun
this ache for wild animals dwindling
into extinction — whose green day
is over.

So many unsaid goodbyes. We are diminished.

A big catalpa blooms at Robson and Cardero,
shading Blockbuster Video.

11 July 1996

Romeo

I sip coffee on the Drive
outside the Romeo. My knees
are sore but improving.

A young guy passes, bouncy
in new boots. Hard to believe
I was once so far from death.

A bum passes: "You're thinking
too much. Don't think,"
he laughs and lurches on.

Brown leaves lie trod flat
or blow by like bus transfers.

28 August 1996

Crow Child

Sparrows squat for a dust-bath
outside Alpha Video, near the cool shade
of a hacked shrub and three kinds of weed.

The Crow Child drags its beak (*sideways,*
head tilted, nostrils foremost) through the bird-bath,
trolling for softened bread-crusts left by its loud
and unremittingly instructive parents.

From below, near the base of the trunk,
the silver maple in Trinity Park
could be a green brain.
                    Delicious — the air
above the great branches, under the leaves!

2 September 1996

A Day

The light at one point had a quality
it was too easy to call pearly: pearl
is duller. It wasn't opalescent either.
More metallic, glancing off the asphalt
on Venables, outside Uprising Bakery.

To the south, a backlit raincloud's bright
hazy corona hundreds of metres deep.

By the time the workers at Core Auto Body
took a morning break, they could sprawl in the shop doorways
in full sun, their blue overalls brown with grinder dust.

When the last rays fell into the Princeton Hotel
the switchman's retirement party was gathering steam
and the Westcoast Express, hauling commuters home,
hammered past, filling the room's back windows.

25 September 1996

Cloud Lifting

Fall clouds have been
dragging sheets of rain

daily across the delta
concealing all heights

until the wind shifts
and clear southern air

fills the valley, drives
the clouds high beyond

the line of rocky peaks
rising north from the green-

sloped harbour, revealing
secret work: electric

white against blue sky — first
snow on the Needles!

6 November 1996

View

An awful muddle near the water: wires
interrupt the sky, the port busily
illustrates Seven Modes of Transportation —

deathy mountain heights snow-clean
a relief in their indifference.

Level late sun
yellows the walls, leaf shadows
flicker and plunge.

7 November 1996

November 11

A pair of T-Bird 33 fighter
jets flew up Burrard Inlet, low

and almost touching, how
war machines pay homage

and terrify. They disappeared
past the Chevron refinery.

The first of eleven rounds
echoed across the water.

Complex, beautiful, rapid, the sky
below Lynn Peak wavered through all

the greys and blues that anyone could want
over forest dark and darker green

and wet for days. Slanting streamers of cloud
drifted across the slopes like smoke.

Ten more cannon rounds,
confused with echoes.

The jets returned and streaked over
the veterans at the cenotaph and the wreaths

at Victory Square and vanished out to sea.
Gradually birds resumed

squabbling and settling and squabbling
and feeding on sunflower seeds:

juncos, fox sparrows, song sparrows,
red-tinged finches, and hateful, beautiful starlings.

11 December 1996

Christmas 1996

for Rita Dahlie

Newspapers and magazines
at first would call the Group of Seven's colours

unlikely; and, in truth, the sun this morning
made the mountain slopes (snow down to the shoreline)

a nearly unbelievable orange: but there it was.

Why did it seem that so much happiness,
such beauty, must be only momentary?

The front ranks are falling
and an enormous effort is required

simply to keep up with the rate of loss.
Like children flinging the first snow into the sky

we pour out energy into the future
and catch occasional crystals as they fall back

through our time: the well-earned weekend, the hike
for the brief luxury of doing nothing but looking;

far across the water, snow outlines each tree.

27 December 1996

Brighten

After a twinge of feeling lost and irrevocably wrong
despite the landscape wherever you are saying
It's all right, dear, I'm here, All right, I'm here,

you look out your front door at the street transformed,
at globes of bare trees glittering with a thousand thousand
sun-brilliant water drops, water lenses sparkling

in rare bright sun, and your spirit rises saying,
despite the jelly ever thickening in your eyes and drifting
tadpole-like across your vision, All right, I'm here.

23 January 1997

So

There, see, a
cloud you could

ride, like a
hippopotamus, no, an

Airedale,
blue, slightly

popeyed yet
noble — gone

on, during
just these

few moments.
I hate feeling

that ephemeral
but it's

true:
you flicker

for a life-
span like a

speeded-up film, you
leave a few old

friends and
books, then

they're gone, then
you're really gone.

Good to be
part of it all

while it lasts.
Best not to

dwell on the
last

too much, it
concentrates the mind

wonderfully but
burns.

So: two sparrows
flirt and plunge

through snowy air,
daffodils ignore the

grass going under
wet white snow.

15 March 1997

Work Animal

What a
fine day, I
murmur to the
daffodils, they
nod under-
standingly,

sea-lions
bark, urgent,
on Rivtow Towing's
barge, step
on one another's
careful phrasings,

a house finch
pours a full
lyric sequence
into grateful
space, which
drinks it.

I must stop
watching the mason
cut chimney
flashing: why
does everyone's
work seem

more important
than mine? Get
to work, animal:
if the laurel flowers
just watched, where
would they be?

No one would see
their beauty,
how their
powdery, palest
yellow pagodas,
festive, celebrate survival.

29 April 1997

Spring Moth

Inches from the freezing rapids
a moth flutters, grey, nearly invisible
against grey rocks. It doesn't fly:
the sun is setting, the air is growing cool

and the moth will wait for tomorrow's sun
to warm it into flight. It walks
over the warm stone fluttering its wings
as if excited by it doesn't know what —

the stone's radiance, yes, and the living works
that drive all creatures on, the gene's clocks, but —
it spreads its incomparably beautiful wings, it looks down
as if pleased with itself, wholly alone.

2 May 1997

Goldenhair

Last summer's grass streams down the mountain slope,
gleams in slanting sunlight almost white,
in tree-shade pale yellow and dappled pink
with fallen orange needles of spruce and pine.
Too dry for nourishment,
it feeds our eyes' hunger
for the beauty of the world, as if it were
the golden hair of a mother who loves us
who is unlimited and everywhere
who smiles up at us and holds us steady
as we learn to walk on her body.

Two deer come over the ridge: one goes on grazing
and one lies down, folding its legs under,
and looks at me, its eyelids slowly closing
— the deer are tired, they have been walking all day
cropping the new green grass — and I am privileged,
I rejoice that in my presence it falls to sleep
as if I were the harmless earth and grass
as one would with a spouse of many years.

6 May 1997

Wind

The small branches
of the young spruce
tremble as the wind pours
over the ridge's crest.

High above,
the older pines
nod, and sway
toward each other: Yes,

this may be the wind
that keeps on rising
till the hush of needles
sifting the air
is a roar, and the weakest

snap, or tear up
roots, and fall.
Yes, they hush
as the sky darkens,
Yes.

9 May 1997

Mid-May

Winter retreats, dragging its snowline
up into the barren rocks.
In the valley the river foams and rises,
roars and clanks ever-larger boulders
along the ribbed brown length of its hurrying belly.

On dry slopes, the forest wakes, stunned and silent:
sharp slants of land, grey verticals of trees
crowded solid with distance; poor, thin ground.

On mossy hillocks, on snow-flattened grass
squirrels scatter showers of woody flakes,
gobbling a new-found wealth of pine cones.

Raking early sun kindles
a dazzling strand of spider web:
later the air will warm, will flicker and waver
with tiny flies, everywhere alive.

Two robins spring into the air, again and again
to struggle against each other, their small down flying.

Each day the forest air grows lovelier
with more and more calls of more various birds;
every morning is sweeter with the damp
infant breath of green unfurling leaves.

16 May 1997

Near Full Moon

The air is soft: scattered patches
of last night's sudden snow — which so amazed
the morning with white forest on white ground —
shrink on wet grass, none larger than a hand.

Clouds mask the peaks, then clear; their frozen
dust has picked out every needled branch
on dark crowded walls of pines. All day
sun followed shade. This evening, light rain.

Mist in even the nearest trees.
Drops tap our faces, upturned to the song
of a robin welcoming rain, content.
These animal trails suit us perfectly.

Reader, as you breathe, in distant
silence, in whatever time or place,
think of us, who have passed through these trees
and gone, like the mule deer, no one knows where.

23 May 1997

Harbour

for Richard Renshaw-Beauchamp, 1926–1997

Plump, flat-bottomed on their cushion
wide as the Fraser Valley, masses of clouds
rub up and down the mountains across the harbour,
wet tendrils infiltrating the dark fir.

The sea mumbles its barnacled shore
(riprap of broken concrete buildings)
down to blue-black bundles of mussels anchored
below rockweed, below the terrible air

we breathe to feed salt blood
and chalk bone, hugging the ache of loss,
proof against an all-surrounding
ocean of crustacean indifference.

17 September 1997

Driver

Rainy morning, a sky so featureless
you have to crane your neck and peer
up through the brightest topmost panes,
fill your head with all available light

just to glimpse a scrap of cloud wrack passing.
A sparrow edges down a twig
that bows near vertical under his weight;
he skates sidelong an inch, eyeing

some morsel near the tip, and grips
to brake his slide, then skids another inch —
what an admirable character,
this acrobat of survival:

one mood all the time! He always feels
like a full hunting and gathering day
in the plum tree's leafless maze
of branches — worm-pink, bird-leg narrow, new.

6 January 1998

Logic Tree

Evenings loud parties of crows fly over
commuting southeast to Burnaby
calling their pleasure in the easy life
down terrifying heights of air.

Most days an eagle swings by
cocking his white helmet
towards the inlet's glint.

What am I looking for, prowling
weedy back lanes blessed with neglect
primitive mouldering board fences,
the scurf of human habitation,
ancient rain forest ghosts?

Rain, dumb parallel
between sky and earth
more palpable than any speech
write your no answer, no answer
between the lines of my hand.

24 March 1998

Arm's Reach

to just light out for the territories
however paved over
yet return constant

as networks of leaf shadow
on the finch-crowded fence

heartbreak evanescing down the lane
banished from under blossoming
cherry's pink igloo

sky earlier improbably clear
now tracered with haze
near the mountainous horizon

the sorceror Juan Matus's advice
think of death as always
perched on your shoulder or
within arm's reach

a wake up call
to direct the attention

a Cates tug
bulls a Gearbulk freighter
across the harbour empty
high floating anvil

new riprap shoreline
broken concrete
sidewalks, the old Pacific National
Exhibition buildings

now greening with
sea lettuce, rockweed,
bull kelp, sea hair

pale clouds of grain dust
drift through harbour water
from Alberta Wheat Pool

freighter sags down
to Plimsoll line at stern
bow still filling
from huge hose-streams of grain

over machinery roar
ship's loudspeaker
speaks in echoing Filipino

small lap of waves on
rocks softened by newgreen blur

truck route behind roars
wheat pool to right roars

Dollarton shipyard
(goodbye Malcolm Lowry
and thanks for the hell)
framed by Second Narrows bridge

four diesel locomotives cross
diagonal black and white
stripes, red head-ends

come on, little blunt guy
get us through this

(a diesel's first job
is self-cooling:
exploding inside, steel
rubs itself liquid, thaws
slumps and jams)

grebe
dives

small wave sound

later that day clouds
catch the full moon

briefly perishing

17 April 1998

Lyric

There's a way to carry it off
that couldn't be more pleasing, but the day
hardens and dries, even the finches' music
attacks like hacksaws. Sunlight is solid

as glass; leaves still gratefully in shadow
shake themselves like wet dogs, like the osprey
springing Venus-like from an unsuccessful plunge,
fatalism written all over it. You can read

too much into such things. It was probably
hungry and busy. Oh, toughen up.
Their refusal to mirror is why we love
dear living things, laurel and pear,

the sleeping cat. The me
has to insist on separateness, horror
that that man trudging the lane, unreadable face,
is our body too, body of earth.

5 May 1998

At the Barricades

When the war of all with all began
I can scarcely remember: is it still on?
I confess I retreat into myself,
"living inside my head", as they say, as if

all manner of things would be well if I would only
stay the hell out of there, and tell the story
we've all heard, and love to hear again,
of the old days, the ones we wish were here.

Of course they're gone, and when they come again
   we'll miss them
just like we did last time, too stuck in our own heads
to catch goings-on that must be reinvented
with each observance. This is how it was:

There was never enough light to hold a day
all the way through: we would grasp a moment, it slipped
away, leaving a sticky residue
of just a leaf, or grass, or ground we knew.

26 June 1998

Muskrat

for Ruth and Mark Phillips

The forest gapes with the white scars of split
and shattered tree trunks after the ice storm,
a death-feast for tiniest creatures
bringing lost life to life again

by feeding on it. You feel helpless here
in the face of disaster on a scale unmatched
except by daily human life, that maw
into which the wild vanishes

however carefully you walk. You watch
the muskrat in the lake as if some silent
lesson was being taught all unawares,
as if its steady singlemindedness

in chewing leaves, in tearing small branchlets
from shrubs, in swimming back along the shore
to feed its hungry young, was something else,
some better way that you could live your life.

5 July 1998

Aspens

The air is packed with water,
full as a lung. Far off, the crump
crump of thunder, not yet frightening.

Remember *The Encyclopedia of the War*,
almost hearing the distant guns,
guns now twice as distant,
forty years on.

The least breeze clatters the aspen leaves.
This weather could go either way.
By afternoon the bay could be alight
with sun on wave-edges, a gnat-dance dazzle,
mesmerizing.

            War is a book to you.
You can sit for hours and watch the water move.
You are living in paradise.

13 July 1998

Split Rock

for John Fraser and Elizabeth McCallum

Thanks to diligent house-
keeping we're free to leave

the airy barnacle
to inventory the island:

Tom Thomson's *West
Wind*'s immortal White Pine

cuttings are thriving youngsters,
the Eastern Red Cedar's

dusty blue juniper
berries gleam like frosty

gin we drink to the Forest
Management Plan's success, its

hands-off husbandry
enriching master, mistress, children,

every tenant in every crevice,
down to the smallest freeholders

whose harmless industry rings
rock-pools with crimson dye.

18 July 1998

Eminent Canadians

for John Fraser

There's an agenda if you see one
say the invisible creatures
whose scarlet scum is painting Georgian Bay
just the way it loves to be painted.
Wasps and small flies feed on the warm pool
blackening as it dries.

All summer an armada of cruisers,
the bigger towing baby bombardiers,
drones up and down the channel;
what is to be done
with these rich boobies, their destructive toys?
Their bloated swells
have sterilized the shoreline.

Still in sheltered bays
you can smell out mucky life,
hear frog-jump-in sound.

21 July 1998
Split Rock Island

NOTES

p. 9 Susan McCabe, *Elizabeth Bishop: Her Poetics of Loss,* Pennsylvania State University Press, 1994.

p. 11 Green Man: "When heads": quoted from a character in Tolkien's *Lord of the Rings,* before setting off through rough country; "plaguey monks": before the invention of the printing press, the first letters of sections of medieval books were elaborately decorated with natural forms and imagery, sometimes by the copyist — no doubt a welcome relief from the tyranny of the alphabet.

p. 12 Lever: "untethered": "To give your sheep or cow a large, spacious meadow is the way to control him" — Shunryu Suzuki, *Zen Mind, Beginner's Mind,* New York, Weatherhill, 1970, p. 32.

p. 17 Immune: "Hope is a chemical": "all this evidence [from medical research] makes it clear that your psychological state can change your immune response. Bereavement, depression and pessimism all can lower your immune system's activity." Martin E.P. Seligman, *Learned Optimism,* Pocket Books, 1990, pp. 178–179.

p. 22 Geranium Lake: Shewfelt Lake is beside Muskoka Road 2, between Huntsville and Baysville, Ontario.

p. 23 Island: Lasqueti Island, BC.

p. 26 Goodbye: "See me": from the Who's rock opera, *Tommy.*

p. 31 Memento: Ayrton Senna died May 1, 1994 in a racing accident during the San Marino Grand Prix.

p. 32 Lions: two mountains of BC's Coast Range, on Vancouver's northern skyline.

p. 37 Mosaic: "Three Babies": Sinead O'Connor's song, from her LP *I do not want what I haven't got,* Chrysalis Records, 1990.

p. 41 Tilt: "no use": "Very little is needed to destroy a man: you need only convince him that his work is useless." — Dostoevsky.

p. 45 For Mir: "VanTerm": a container terminal in the Port of Vancouver.

p. 48 For Tu Fu: "Two Sisters": from an aboriginal name for the Lions.

p. 49 "Everything's Going My Way": titled from the Queers' song, from their LP *Move Back Home,* Lookout Records, 1995.

p. 57 Christmas 1996: early reviews of the Group of Seven's paintings can be found among the 300,000 volumes of the Vancouver Public Library's Newspapers and Magazines Division. I am indebted to the head of the Division, Rita Dahlie, for line eight.

p. 59 So: "Depend upon it, Sir, when a man knows he is to be hanged in a fortnight, it concentrates his mind wonderfully." Samuel Johnson, in Boswell's *Life,* 19 September 1777.

p. 79 Eminent Canadians: "frog-jump-in sound": this is a reference to Matsuo Basho's poem of 1686, probably the best-known haiku in the Japanese language.

ABOUT THE AUTHOR

John Donlan was raised in Baysville, a hamlet of 200 people in Ontario's Muskoka district on the Canadian Shield. His father worked with teams of horses hauling logs in the bush; neighbours raised skunks, crows and porcupines as domestic pets. Surrounded by some of Canada's most beautiful wilderness, celebrated in the paintings of Tom Thomson and the Group of Seven, he developed a deep sense of belonging in the natural world. He began writing poetry and publishing in literary magazines in the 1960s. He has worked as a reference librarian since 1974, and in 1987 became a poetry editor with Brick Books. He lives in Vancouver with his wife, Miriam Clavir, and their three cats. He subsidizes his poetry career with a part-time position in the Newspapers and Magazines Division of the Vancouver Public Library.